LOVE UNDER PRESSURE WORKBOOK

GUIDED EXERCISES FOR MARITAL RESILIENCE, SPOUSAL SUPPORT, AND THE SCIENCE OF SHARED STRESS

PRINCE-JAMES SMITH, PHD

A Guided Companion to Love Under Pressure

LOVE UNDER PRESSURE WORKBOOK

This workbook is educational and reflective. It is not a substitute for therapy, medical care, legal guidance, crisis intervention, or other professional services. Readers experiencing relationship abuse, coercion, threats, violence, severe emotional distress, self-harm thoughts, or safety concerns should seek immediate support from qualified professionals, emergency services, or appropriate crisis resources.

Quantity sales and special discounts are available on quantity purchases by corporations, associations, and others. For details, contact the publisher at the address above.

Orders by U.S. trade bookstores and wholesalers. Email Michael@BeyondPublishing.net

The Beyond Publishing Speakers Bureau can bring authors to your live event. For more information or to book an event contact the Beyond Publishing Speakers Bureau speak@BeyondPublishing.net

The Author can be reached directly at BeyondPublishing.net

Manufactured and printed in the United States of America distributed globally by BeyondPublishing.net

BEYOND
PUBLISHING

New York / Los Angeles / London / Sydney / Bangkok

ISBN: 979-8-9962262-4-5

DEDICATION

To the next generation of lovers.

May you inherit more than stories about love. May you inherit the courage, discipline, humility, and wisdom to build relationships that are not only passionate, but steady; not only beautiful in public, but safe in private; not only emotionally meaningful, but resilient under pressure.

Alexis, Chris, Micah, Mateo, Princess, Malik, Tony, and Prince; learning to love starts with self-love and personal mastery. May your transformation in love be fruitful

TABLE OF CONTENTS

PREFACE

WHY THIS BOOK HAD TO BE WRITTEN

This workbook was created for the moments when love needs more than understanding. It was created for the moments when a couple can see that pressure has entered the relationship, but they do not yet know how to name what is happening, how to support each other, or how to stop the stressor from quietly becoming the center of the marriage. The companion book, Love Under Pressure, explains the psychology, research, and relationship framework behind shared stress, marital resilience, spousal support, dyadic coping, emotional regulation, communication, repair, and role adjustment. This workbook turns those ideas into guided practice.

The purpose of this workbook is not to diagnose your relationship, judge your marriage, or force every couple into the same pattern of healing. Relationships are living systems, and no two systems carry pressure in exactly the same way. Some couples arrive here while facing financial strain. Some are managing illness, grief, parenting stress, caregiving, work demands, infertility, relocation, family conflict, or emotional exhaustion. Some are not in crisis at all, but they want to prepare for pressure before the next difficult season arrives. Wherever you begin, the work is the same in principle: name the pressure, understand its effect, clarify support, protect emotional safety, repair harm, and take the next small step in the right direction.

This workbook is grounded in a simple but demanding belief: resilience is the choice to show up through intentional actions in the present moment. It is shaped through small steps in the right direction. Resilience is not perfection. It is not emotional toughness. It is not staying silent to keep the peace. It is not pretending that harm is acceptable because life is difficult. Resilience requires honesty, accountability, dignity, emotional safety, support, repair, and the willingness to learn from what pressure reveals.

The exercises in these pages are designed to slow the relationship down. Shared stress often creates speed. Partners react quickly, assume quickly, defend quickly, withdraw quickly, or blame quickly. This workbook asks you to pause long enough to see the system more clearly. What is the shared stressor? How is it affecting each partner differently? What resources are being depleted? What kind of support is being offered, and what kind is actually needed? What communication patterns are protecting the relationship, and which ones are making pressure heavier? What roles have changed silently? What needs repair? What needs outside support?

Some readers will complete this workbook with a spouse or partner. Others will complete it alone first, either because their partner is not ready, because they need personal clarity before beginning a conversation, or because they are trying to understand what happened during a difficult season. Both uses are valid. A relationship can begin to change when one person becomes more aware of the system, their own patterns, their needs, their boundaries, and the support they are willing and able to offer. At the same time, this workbook does not place the full burden of relationship repair on one partner. Relational resilience requires participation. One person can begin reflection, but one person cannot do the entire work of mutual accountability, safety, and repair alone.

This workbook is educational and reflective. It is not a substitute for therapy, medical care, legal guidance, crisis intervention, or professional support. If your relationship includes abuse, intimidation, coercion, threats, violence, severe emotional harm, fear of retaliation, or patterns that make honesty unsafe, ordinary communication exercises may not be appropriate. In those situations, the priority is safety, protection, and qualified support. Love under pressure must never become a reason to remain in danger.

Use these pages with patience. Some exercises may feel straightforward. Others may reveal tension, grief, resentment, fatigue, or disappointment that has been carried quietly for a long time. Move slowly when needed. Return to the exercises more than once. Do not use the prompts as weapons. Do not use them to prove that one partner is the problem. Use them to understand the relationship system, clarify what must change, and decide what kind of love you are willing to practice while pressure is real.

HOW TO USE THIS WORKBOOK

This workbook is designed as a guided companion to Love Under Pressure, but it can also be used as a stand-alone resource for individuals and couples who want to strengthen relationship resilience during shared stress. Each chapter introduces one core relationship concept, then moves into reflective exercises, guided prompts, and practical commitments. The exercises are not meant to be rushed. They are designed to help you think, feel, discuss, and act with more clarity.

You may use this workbook in three ways. You may complete it individually to better understand your own stress responses, needs, support patterns, and boundaries. You may complete it as a couple, working through each chapter together and using the prompts as structured conversations. You may also use it after reading each chapter of Love Under Pressure, allowing the book to provide the deeper explanation and the workbook to provide application.

If you are completing this workbook as a couple, begin with an agreement that the exercises will not be used to attack, shame, diagnose, or corner each other. The purpose is not to win an argument. The purpose is to understand what pressure is doing to the relationship and what each partner can do to protect the bond with greater intention. If a conversation becomes too intense, pause. A responsible pause is not avoidance when both partners agree to return. Write down when you will resume the conversation and honor that commitment.

If you are completing this workbook alone, answer honestly without using the exercises to build a private case against your partner. Reflection should create clarity, not contempt. Notice your own needs, but also notice your own patterns. How do you communicate stress? How do you ask for support? What kind of support do you tend to offer? What happens when you feel overwhelmed? What do you avoid? What do you need to repair? What boundaries are necessary for your emotional safety? These questions matter even when the other partner is not yet participating.

Each chapter follows a consistent rhythm. First, you will be invited into the concept through a brief teaching section. Then you will complete guided exercises. Some exercises are reflective. Some are conversational. Some ask for concrete action. Some ask you to make agreements. At the end of each chapter, you will identify a small step in the right direction. This step matters. Relationship resilience is not built only through insight. It is built when insight becomes behavior.

Several exercises use Acceptance and Commitment Therapy (ACT)-informed language, especially values, psychological flexibility, acceptance, defusion, and committed action. In this workbook, these ideas are used educationally to help partners notice difficult thoughts and feelings without automatically obeying them, return to what matters, and choose behavior that protects the relationship while pressure is present (Hayes et al., 2012).

You do not need to complete the workbook in order, though the order is intentional. The early chapters help you name shared pressure and understand the relationship as a system. The middle chapters focus on support, coping, emotional regulation, communication, and role adjustment. The later chapters focus on repair, reconnection, crisis planning, and outside support. If you are currently facing a specific crisis, you may begin with the Shared Stressor Crisis Plan and return to the earlier chapters afterward.

A NOTE ON SAFETY AND PROFESSIONAL SUPPORT

This workbook is intended for relationships where both partners are willing to engage in honesty, accountability, emotional safety, and repair. It is not designed to help someone tolerate abuse, coercion, intimidation, violence, severe emotional degradation, threats, or fear. If any exercise makes you feel unsafe because of how your partner may react, do not complete that exercise together without appropriate professional guidance.

There is an important difference between pressure and danger. Pressure may involve stress, fatigue, conflict, fear, grief, uncertainty, or emotional strain. Danger involves patterns that threaten a person's safety, dignity, autonomy, or freedom. Physical violence, threats of harm, coercive control, stalking, financial control used to trap or punish, sexual coercion, intimidation, forced isolation, destruction of property, and repeated humiliation are not ordinary relationship stress. These situations require safety planning and qualified support.

Seeking help is not a failure. Couples therapy, individual therapy, medical care, legal guidance, financial counseling, pastoral care, community resources, or crisis services may be necessary depending on the situation. A resilient relationship does not prove its strength by refusing support. It proves its maturity by knowing when support is needed.

PART ONE

UNDERSTANDING SHARED PRESSURE

CHAPTER 1

NAMING THE SHARED STRESSOR

Pressure becomes more powerful when it remains unnamed. Many couples argue around a stressor long before they identify it directly. They argue about the tone, the schedule, the bill, the dishes, the child, the appointment, the silence, the spending, the family member, or the missed task. Those issues may be real, but they may also be the visible surface of a deeper shared pressure. Until the couple names the pressure clearly, each partner may begin to experience the other as the problem.

A shared stressor is any pressure that affects both partners and requires the relationship to adapt. It does not have to affect both people in the same way. In fact, it usually will not. One partner may experience a financial stressor as fear, while the other experiences it as shame. One may experience caregiving as duty, while the other experiences it as emotional exhaustion. The stressor is shared because both partners are affected, both must respond, and the relationship itself becomes part of the system under strain. The companion book is informed by qualitative research on marital resilience, spousal support, and shared stressors in long-term marriages (Smith, 2026).

Naming the stressor is the first act of relational clarity. Stress research emphasizes that people respond not only to events themselves, but also to how they appraise those events and evaluate their available resources (Lazarus & Folkman, 1984). In marriage, appraisal becomes relational because each partner is also interpreting the other partner's response to the pressure. Research on couples and stress suggests that external stress can spill into relationship functioning, influencing conflict, satisfaction, coping, and emotional connection (Randall & Bodenmann, 2009). A couple that can name pressure has a better chance of not collapsing the entire crisis into one person's character.

This first chapter begins the workbook by helping you identify the pressure you are actually facing. The goal is not to solve it immediately. The goal is to name it with enough clarity that both partners can begin responding with intention rather than reflex.

CORE TEACHING

Shared pressure can make partners believe they should understand each other automatically because they are living through the same event. That belief often fails. Two partners can occupy the same crisis and still carry different losses, fears, meanings, and needs. Family resilience research emphasizes that adaptation during adversity depends partly on meaning making, communication, flexibility, and relational processes rather than the absence of adversity itself (Walsh, 2016). Naming the stressor gives the couple a place to begin that process.

A clear stressor name should be specific enough to guide action. 'We are stressed' is true, but it may not help. 'We are facing financial instability after a job loss, and it is affecting our sleep, communication, and sense of safety' gives the couple more useful information. 'We are caregiving for an aging parent, and the time demands are changing our roles and draining our emotional energy' gives the relationship something concrete to organize around. Dyadic coping research also reminds couples that stress becomes relational when partners communicate stress, respond to each other's stress, and coordinate coping efforts together (Bodenmann, 2005).

Naming pressure does not erase accountability. If a partner has spoken harshly, withdrawn, controlled, avoided responsibility, or caused harm, that behavior still needs to be addressed. The purpose of naming the stressor is to widen the lens, not to excuse harm. A couple can say, 'This stressor is affecting us,' and also say, 'The way we are treating each other inside this stressor must change.'

GUIDED EXERCISE

THE SHARED STRESSOR NAMING PRACTICE

Complete this exercise slowly. If you are working as a couple, answer individually first, then discuss the overlap and differences.

Reflection Prompt	Response / Notes
The shared stressor I believe we are facing is:	
What makes this stressor shared is:	
This stressor entered our relationship through:	
This stressor affects our daily life by changing:	
This stressor affects our emotional connection by changing:	
This stressor affects our communication by changing:	

Reflection Prompt	Response / Notes
This stressor affects our roles or responsibilities by changing:	
This stressor affects our sense of safety, stability, or hope by changing:	
The part of this stressor we can influence is:	
The part of this stressor we cannot fully control is:	

PARTNER REFLECTION

Use these prompts to distinguish your personal experience from the shared event.

Reflection Prompt	Response / Notes
The stressor feels most difficult for me because:	
The emotion I feel most often around this stressor is:	
The thought I keep having about this stressor is:	

Reflection Prompt	Response / Notes
What I wish my partner understood about my experience is:	
What I may not have communicated clearly is:	
One way I may be reacting to the stressor instead of responding intentionally is:	

COUPLE CONVERSATION

WHAT ARE WE REALLY FACING?

Begin with the sentence, "The shared stressor we are facing is..." Then use the prompts below.

Reflection Prompt	Response / Notes
Where do our answers overlap?	
Where do our answers differ?	
What did one partner name that the other partner had not fully noticed?	
What have we been arguing about that may actually be connected to this deeper stressor?	

Reflection Prompt	Response / Notes
How has this stressor changed the emotional climate of our relationship?	
How has this stressor changed what each of us needs?	
What do we need to stop blaming each other for that may actually be pressure acting on the relationship?	
What behavior still needs accountability, even if pressure helps explain it?	

MALL STEP IN THE RIGHT DIRECTION

The goal is not to fix the whole stressor. The goal is to name it clearly enough to begin responding differently.

Reflection Prompt	Response / Notes
One small step I can take to name pressure before blaming my partner is:	
One small step we can take as a couple to face the stressor more clearly is:	
We will revisit this conversation on:	

CLOSING REFLECTION

A shared stressor becomes more dangerous when it remains unnamed. Without a name, it moves through the relationship as irritation, distance, criticism, anxiety, silence, or resentment. Once named, it becomes something the couple can observe. It may still be difficult, painful, or complex, but it is no longer operating entirely in the dark. Naming the stressor is the first small step in the right direction.

CHAPTER 2

THE RELATIONSHIP AS A SYSTEM UNDER STRAIN

A relationship under pressure is never only two individuals feeling stress at the same time. It is a system responding to strain. One partner's silence affects the other's sense of safety. One partner's urgency affects the other's nervous system. One partner's over-functioning may invite the other partner's under-functioning. The relationship begins to produce patterns, and those patterns can become stronger than either partner's intentions.

Systems thinking asks us to look beyond isolated events and examine patterns, connections, feedback loops, and the way one part of a system shapes another (Senge, 1990). Family systems theory similarly emphasizes that individual behavior is best understood within relational patterns, roles, boundaries, and structures (Minuchin, 1974). In marriage, this means the visible conflict is often only one part of a larger system strain.

CORE TEACHING

Many couples interpret pressure through the narrowest behavior. A partner withdraws, so the issue is withdrawal. A partner criticizes, so the issue is criticism. A partner takes over, so the issue is control. These behaviors matter, and they may need repair. But a systems view asks what conditions keep making those behaviors more likely. Is the couple exhausted? Is role imbalance increasing? Are decisions happening too late at night? Has one partner become the informal manager of every crisis? Has emotional safety been weakened by repeated arguments without repair?

A systems lens does not remove personal responsibility. It makes responsibility more accurate. Instead of saying, 'You are the problem,' a couple can begin to ask, 'What pattern are we caught in, and what are each of us doing that keeps it alive?' This question opens the possibility of change. It helps partners move from accusation to pattern recognition.

Shared stress often drains the very resources couples need in order to respond well. Conservation of Resources theory suggests that stress intensifies when valued resources are threatened, lost, or not sufficiently restored (Hobfoll, 1989). In relationships, those resources include time, sleep, emotional energy, attention, trust, hope, privacy, patience, and decision-making capacity. When the relationship is under-resourced, partners may misread depletion as lack of love.

GUIDED EXERCISE

SYSTEM STRAIN MAP

Use this map to identify where pressure is entering the relationship system.

Reflection Prompt	Response / Notes
The shared stressor is showing up in our daily routine through:	
The stressor is showing up in our communication through:	
The stressor is showing up in our emotional connection through:	
The stressor is showing up in our physical bodies or health through:	
The stressor is showing up in our parenting, caregiving, or family roles through:	
The stressor is showing up in our finances or practical responsibilities through:	
The stressor is showing up in our intimacy or affection through:	
The stressor is showing up in our sense of hope, trust, or safety through:	

PATTERN RECOGNITION

Do not use these prompts to blame. Use them to see what the system is repeatedly producing.

Reflection Prompt	Response / Notes
A pattern we repeat when pressure rises is:	
Partner One often responds by:	
Partner Two often responds by:	
This creates a cycle where:	
The cycle usually escalates when:	
The cycle usually softens when:	
One condition that keeps this pattern alive is:	
One condition we could change is:	

SMALL STEP IN THE RIGHT DIRECTION

Choose one system condition to adjust this week.

Reflection Prompt	Response / Notes
One pattern we want to interrupt is:	
One condition we can change this week is:	
The specific action we will take is:	
We will check whether it helped on:	

CLOSING REFLECTION

The relationship will organize around something when pressure enters. It may organize around fear, blame, silence, control, or avoidance. With intention, it can also organize around clarity, support, flexibility, and repair. Seeing the relationship as a system under strain helps partners stop treating every painful moment as proof that the relationship is broken and begin asking what the system needs in order to function more wisely.

CHAPTER 3

MAPPING RESOURCE DEPLETION

Couples often argue about behavior when the deeper issue is depletion. The conversation sounds like it is about tone, chores, money, intimacy, or parenting, but underneath the conflict there may be too little sleep, too little time, too little patience, too little trust, too little emotional energy, or too little hope. When resources are depleted, ordinary relationship demands feel heavier.

Resource depletion matters because stress is not only the presence of a demand. It is also the experience of not having enough resources to meet that demand. Conservation of Resources theory provides a useful framework for understanding why threat, loss, and insufficient restoration of valued resources can intensify stress (Hobfoll, 1989). In a relationship, resources are practical, emotional, physical, relational, and social.

CORE TEACHING

A couple under pressure must ask what is being drained before depletion becomes blame. If sleep is depleted, serious conversations may become more volatile. If trust is depleted, small ambiguities may feel dangerous. If time is depleted, affection may disappear not because love is absent, but because the couple has not protected space for connection. If hope is depleted, partners may become cynical, passive, or cruel because they no longer believe their effort matters.

Resource awareness is not an excuse for harmful behavior. It is an intervention point. A partner who is exhausted still has responsibility for how they speak. A partner who is anxious still has responsibility not to control. A partner who is ashamed still has responsibility not to blame. But when the couple can identify what is depleted, it can respond more accurately. A depleted resource needs protection, restoration, or outside support.

GUIDED EXERCISE

RELATIONSHIP RESOURCE INVENTORY

Mark each resource as strong, strained, depleted, or needing restoration. Use the notes column to explain why.

Reflection Prompt	Response / Notes
Time:	
Money:	
Sleep:	
Physical health:	
Mental health:	
Emotional energy:	
Patience:	
Trust:	
Communication:	
Decision-making capacity:	
Affection:	
Sexual intimacy:	
Privacy:	
Hope:	
Confidence:	
Sense of safety:	
Social or family support:	
Shared meaning:	

MOST DEPLETED RESOURCES

Identify what needs the most immediate attention.

Reflection Prompt	Response / Notes
The three resources most depleted right now are:	
The signs that these resources are depleted are:	
This depletion affects Partner One by:	
This depletion affects Partner Two by:	
This depletion affects the relationship by:	
The resource most urgent to protect is:	
The resource most urgent to restore is:	

RESOURCE PROTECTION PLAN

Reduce unnecessary loss and protect what remains.

Reflection Prompt	Response / Notes
A demand we need to reduce is:	
A responsibility we need to simplify is:	
A task we need to delegate is:	
A conversation we need to schedule more wisely is:	
A boundary we need to set with others is:	
A habit that is draining us is:	
A habit that could protect us is:	

SMALL STEP IN THE RIGHT DIRECTION

Choose one resource to protect this week and one resource to restore.

Reflection Prompt	Response / Notes
For the next week, we agree to protect:	
For the next week, we agree to restore:	
Partner One will take responsibility for:	
Partner Two will take responsibility for:	
We will reduce, postpone, or delegate:	
We will review this resource plan on:	

PART TWO

SUPPORT UNDER STRESS

CHAPTER 4

NAMING THE SHARED STRESSOR

Support is one of the most familiar words in the language of marriage, yet familiarity can make the word imprecise. One partner may hear support and think of emotional presence. Another may think of practical help. Another may think of loyalty, advice, protection, reassurance, advocacy, or shared planning. Under pressure, these differences matter because support that is sincere may still fail to land.

Social support research distinguishes between the support that is actually provided and the support that is perceived as available, meaningful, and helpful (Cutrona, 1996; Haber et al., 2007). This distinction is essential in marriage. A partner may insist, 'I helped,' while the other responds, 'I still felt alone.' Both may be telling a truth from different positions.

CORE TEACHING

Support includes the act, but it also includes the message carried by the act. A partner may complete a task, but if the task is done with resentment or superiority, it may not feel supportive. A partner may offer kind words, but if practical responsibilities remain unchanged, the words may feel insufficient. Under shared stress, support must become visible, specific, responsive, and usable.

Support is also relational history. A supportive act is received through past experiences of reliability, disappointment, repair, gratitude, resentment, and trust. A partner who has often been emotionally available may be given grace during a tired moment. A partner who has repeatedly dismissed vulnerability may find that even sincere support is received with caution. This does not make repair impossible, but it means support must become consistent enough to rebuild credibility.

Dyadic coping research suggests that how couples respond to stress together is associated with relationship satisfaction and relational functioning (Bodenmann, 2005; Falconier et al., 2015). Support is one of the clearest ways dyadic coping becomes visible. It tells the partner, 'You are not alone in this, even though I am struggling too.'

GUIDED EXERCISE

SUPPORT TYPE INVENTORY

Identify which forms of support matter most under pressure.

Reflection Prompt	Response / Notes
Emotional support helps me when:	
Practical support helps me when:	
Informational support or advice helps me when:	
Esteem support protects my dignity when:	
Regulatory support helps me calm down when:	
Presence-based support helps me feel less alone when:	
Shared planning support helps me when:	
The type of support I need most right now is:	

SUPPORT I TEND TO OFFER

Many people offer the kind of support they prefer to receive. Use this exercise to examine your default pattern.

Reflection Prompt	Response / Notes
When my partner is under pressure, I usually offer support by:	
The kind of support I offer most easily is:	
The kind of support I struggle to offer is:	
I tend to avoid offering support when:	
I may think I am helping when I am actually:	
One way I want to become more responsive as a support partner is:	
One question I can ask before assuming what support is needed is:	

SUPPORT I STRUGGLE TO RECEIVE

Some people need support but struggle to accept it. Explore what makes receiving support difficult.

Reflection Prompt	Response / Notes
I struggle to receive support when:	
When my partner tries to help, I sometimes:	
Receiving support makes me feel:	
The type of support that feels easiest to receive is:	
The type of support that feels hardest to receive is:	
One reason support may be hard for me to accept is:	
One way I can become more open to support is:	

STEP IN THE RIGHT DIRECTION

Make one support request specific enough to guide behavior.

Reflection Prompt	Response / Notes
When I am under pressure, support looks like:	
One support action I will ask for more clearly this week is:	
One support action I will offer more intentionally this week is:	

CHAPTER 5

TRANSLATING MISREAD OR MISALIGNED SUPPORT

Support does not fail only when it is absent. Sometimes support fails because it arrives in a form the other partner cannot recognize, cannot use, or cannot trust. A person can care deeply and still miss the need in front of them. A person can make an effort and still leave the other partner feeling alone.

The gap between intended support and experienced support is one of the most important pressure points in marriage. Received support and perceived support are not the same thing, and perceived support can be especially important to how people experience stress and security (Haber et al., 2007).

CORE TEACHING

Misalignment often begins because partners give the support they themselves would want. A partner who calms through problem solving may offer advice quickly. A partner who calms through expression may want extended conversation. A partner who regulates through solitude may offer space. A partner who regulates through closeness may check in repeatedly. None of these responses is automatically wrong. The problem emerges when the giver assumes their preferred support style is universally supportive.

Support is also filtered through attachment, history, and expectation. Close relationships shape expectations of availability, responsiveness, and safety, especially in distress (Bowlby, 1969; Mikulincer & Shaver, 2016). A partner who has often felt dismissed may hear advice as criticism. A partner who has often felt controlled may experience help as intrusion. A partner who has often felt abandoned may interpret space as rejection. Translation does not mean every interpretation is accurate. It means the relationship must take interpretation seriously enough to clarify it.

A support translation question can prevent many injuries: 'Do you need comfort, solutions, space, or action?' This question is simple, but it changes the emotional process. It turns support from an assumption into a conversation.

GUIDED EXERCISE

INTENTION AND IMPACT

Use this exercise to examine a recent support mismatch without turning it into blame.

Reflection Prompt	Response / Notes
The situation where support did not land well was:	
The support that was offered was:	
The intention behind the support may have been:	
The impact on the receiver was:	
What the receiver needed first was:	
What the giver needed to understand was:	
What could be tried differently next time is:	

COMFORT, SOLUTIONS, SPACE, OR ACTION

Complete the prompts to clarify what each support type means in your relationship.

Reflection Prompt	Response / Notes
Comfort is helpful when:	
Solutions are helpful when:	

Reflection Prompt	Response / Notes
Space is helpful when:	
Action is helpful when:	
Comfort is not helpful when:	
Solutions are not helpful when:	
Space is not helpful when:	
Action is not helpful when:	

SUPPORT TRANSLATION AGREEMENT

Create language that helps support reach the person it is meant to help.

Reflection Prompt	Response / Notes
Before offering support, we can ask:	
When I need comfort before solutions, I can say:	
When I need practical help, I can say:	

Reflection Prompt	Response / Notes
When I need space without abandonment, I can say:	
When I need action instead of reassurance, I can say:	
When I appreciate the effort but need a different kind of support, I can say:	

CLOSING REFLECTION

When support is misread or misaligned, couples do not have to conclude that love is absent. Often, love needs translation. The giver may need to adjust form, tone, timing, or follow-through. The receiver may need to clarify need more directly. Both partners may need to remember that support under pressure is not proven by effort alone, but by whether the effort reaches the person it was meant to help.

CHAPTER 6

BUILDING A SHARED SUPPORT LANGUAGE

A shared support language allows couples to ask for help without relying on mind reading. It also helps partners offer care without guessing. Under pressure, guessing becomes risky because stress changes needs. The partner who usually wants space may need closeness this time. The partner who usually wants advice may need reassurance first. The support language that worked in one season may need revision in another.

Support becomes more useful when it is specific. 'Be there for me' is emotionally true, but it may be too vague to guide behavior under stress. 'Sit with me for ten minutes before offering solutions' is more usable. 'Take ownership of the school communication this week' is more usable. 'Ask me whether I want comfort or action before you respond' is more usable.

CORE TEACHING

Shared language is a relational tool. It gives the couple a way to communicate need before the need becomes accusation. It also helps partners maintain dignity. A clear support request is different from a demand, a test, or a complaint. It invites participation. It gives the partner an opportunity to respond accurately. Research on spousal support shows that the perceived helpfulness of support depends on support type, context, and the receiver's experience of the exchange (Xu & Burleson, 2001; Haber et al., 2007).

The support language should include both needs and limits. Under shared stress, both partners may be depleted. A partner may say, 'I want to support you, and I have capacity for one task tonight, not a long conversation.' This kind of capacity honesty protects the relationship from overpromising, underdelivering, and building resentment.

GUIDED EXERCISE

PARTNER DISTRESS AWARENESS MAP

Support often begins before a request is spoken. When partners learn to notice early signs of distress, they can intervene before one person carries the entire load alone. Stress can spill into relationship functioning and change communication, patience, and support patterns (Randall & Bodenmann, 2009). Perceived support also matters, because a partner may feel more secure when support is noticed as available and responsive before distress becomes overwhelming (Haber et al., 2007).

This exercise is not about mind reading or diagnosing your partner. It is about becoming more observant, asking better questions, and responding earlier with care. Complete it individually first, then compare your answers if it is safe to do so.

Reflection Prompt	Response / Notes
When my partner is under distress, I often notice these facial or body cues:	
When my partner is under distress, I often notice these changes in tone, words, or silence:	
When my partner is under distress, I often notice these changes in routine, attention, or follow-through:	
The distress cue I sometimes miss or misread is:	
The cue that tells me my partner may need immediate relief from the load is:	
When I notice distress, the question I can ask before assuming is:	

Reflection Prompt	Response / Notes
One small support action I can offer without taking over is:	
One responsibility I can temporarily carry when my partner is stabilizing is:	
One sign that outside or professional support may be needed is:	

EARLY LOAD-LIGHTENING PRACTICE

Awareness should lead to a small, practical intervention. The goal is not to rescue the other partner or erase their agency. The goal is to reduce preventable strain before distress turns into resentment, shutdown, or escalation.

Reflection Prompt	Response / Notes
The recurring stress cue we want to notice earlier is:	
When this cue appears, the first partner will say:	
The second partner will respond by:	
The task, decision, or emotional load that can be lightened is:	
We will check whether the intervention helped by asking:	

GUIDED EXERCISE: MY SUPPORT DICTIONARY

Define the phrases you want your partner to understand when you are under pressure.

Reflection Prompt	Response / Notes
When I say, "I am overwhelmed," I usually mean:	
When I say, "I need space," I usually mean:	
When I say, "I need support," I usually mean:	
When I say, "I do not know what I need," I usually need:	
When I go quiet, what may be happening internally is:	
When I become urgent, what may be happening internally is:	
When I ask repeated questions, what may be happening internally is:	
When I seem distant, what may be happening internally is:	

COUPLE SUPPORT SIGNALS

Create short phrases that help each partner request support clearly.

Reflection Prompt	Response / Notes
Our phrase for comfort before solutions will be:	
Our phrase for needing practical help will be:	
Our phrase for needing a pause with return will be:	
Our phrase for needing shared planning will be:	
Our phrase for needing reassurance will be:	
Our phrase for needing outside support will be:	
Our phrase for recognizing support that landed well will be:	

WEEKLY SUPPORT PRACTICE

Use this practice once each week during a stressful season.

Reflection Prompt	Response / Notes
What felt heaviest for you this week?	
Where did you feel supported?	
Where did support miss or feel absent?	
What support do you need next week?	
What support can I realistically offer next week?	
What support do we need from outside the relationship?	

CLOSING REFLECTION

A shared support language is not a script that removes uncertainty from marriage. It is a way of reducing unnecessary confusion. It teaches the couple to ask earlier, clarify faster, and repair support mismatches before they become proof that the other person does not care.

PART THREE

COPING AND COMMUNICATION

CHAPTER 7

FROM SELF-COPING TO DYADIC AND BIDIRECTIONAL COPING

Every person enters a relationship with a history of coping. Some people talk through distress. Some go quiet. Some plan, fix, research, avoid, appease, or take control. These patterns may begin as personal survival strategies, but in marriage they are never entirely private. Under shared stress, the couple must move from solo coping to dyadic coping, and then into bidirectional load-sharing: a flexible process where each partner may temporarily carry more of the relational or practical weight while the other stabilizes.

Dyadic coping refers to the ways couples communicate stress, respond to each other's stress, and manage stress together as a relational unit (Bodenmann, 2005). Research suggests that dyadic coping is associated with relationship satisfaction and relational functioning, especially when couples face stress (Falconier et al., 2015; Randall & Bodenmann, 2009). Bidirectional coping extends this practice by recognizing that support may need to move back and forth across the couple as capacity changes.

CORE TEACHING

Self-coping asks, 'What do I need to do to manage my own distress?' Dyadic coping asks, 'How does the way I manage my distress affect the person beside me, and how can we coordinate our responses so that the stressor does not divide us?' Both questions matter. Adults remain responsible for self-awareness and emotional regulation. At the same time, committed relationships require partners to recognize that coping styles have relational consequences.

Coping collisions happen when each partner's stress response activates the other partner's stress response. The partner who needs closeness moves closer. The partner who needs space moves away. The partner who needs information asks more questions. The partner overwhelmed by information shuts down. Without a shared language, the couple may interpret coping differences as lack of care, control, neediness, or rejection.

GUIDED EXERCISE

PERSONAL COPING PATTERN

Answer individually first. Then discuss how each coping pattern affects the relationship.

Reflection Prompt	Response / Notes
When I am under stress, I usually cope by:	
This coping pattern developed because:	
This coping pattern helps me by:	
This coping pattern can hurt the relationship when:	
What I need my partner to understand about this coping pattern is:	
One thing I am willing to adjust is:	
One thing I need my partner to adjust in response is:	

COPING COLLISION MAP

Use this exercise to understand the cycle without blaming either partner as the whole problem.

Reflection Prompt	Response / Notes
Our most common coping collision is:	
When Partner One copes by:	
Partner Two tends to respond by:	
When Partner Two copes by:	
Partner One tends to respond by:	
This creates a cycle where:	
The feeling underneath Partner One's response is often:	
The feeling underneath Partner Two's response is often:	
The need underneath Partner One's response is often:	
The need underneath Partner Two's response is often:	

COMMON COPING AGREEMENT

Common coping happens when both partners face the stressor together without erasing individual responsibility.

Reflection Prompt	Response / Notes
The shared stressor we need to face together is:	
The part of this stressor we can manage together is:	
The part each partner needs to handle individually is:	
The part we need outside help with is:	
Our next shared action step is:	
Our shared coping agreement for this week is:	
We will revisit this agreement on:	

GUIDED EXERCISE

BIDIRECTIONAL LOAD-SHARING PLAN

Shared stress rarely produces equal capacity in both partners at every moment. Bidirectional load-sharing means the couple agrees that one partner may temporarily carry more practical, emotional, or decision-making weight while the other stabilizes, and then the pattern can reverse when capacity changes. This is not scorekeeping. It is flexible dyadic coping with accountability (Bodenmann, 2005; Falconier et al., 2015).

Temporary imbalance becomes dangerous when it is invisible, assumed, or never revisited. A healthier pattern names the imbalance, appreciates the partner carrying more, protects the stabilizing partner's dignity, and sets a review point so temporary support does not become permanent obligation.

Reflection Prompt	Response / Notes
During this shared stressor, Partner One may need extra support when:	
When Partner One is stabilizing, Partner Two can temporarily carry:	
During this shared stressor, Partner Two may need extra support when:	
When Partner Two is stabilizing, Partner One can temporarily carry:	
The sign that capacity is beginning to return is:	
The sign that the current load-sharing arrangement is becoming unsustainable is:	
The appreciation or pleasantry we will use when one partner carries more is:	
The date or condition when we will revisit this arrangement is:	
If neither partner has enough capacity, the outside support we will seek is:	

STABILIZATION CHECK-IN

Use this check-in during active pressure. It helps partners move from asking, 'Why are you not carrying your part?' to asking, 'What is your capacity right now, and how do we keep the load from crushing either of us?'

Reflection Prompt	Response / Notes
Today, my capacity is best described as:	
The part of the load I can carry today is:	
The part of the load I cannot carry today is:	
The support I need while I stabilize is:	
The support I can still offer you is:	
One small step we can take together today is:	

CHAPTER 8

EMOTIONAL REGULATION WHEN BOTH PARTNERS ARE STRUGGLING

Pressure does not only change what couples face. It changes how they face it. A conversation that would have been manageable in a calmer season may become explosive when both partners are tired. A small delay in response may feel like rejection. A practical question may sound like criticism. Under shared stress, partners communicate through nervous systems that may already be activated, depleted, guarded, or overwhelmed.

Emotion regulation refers to the processes by which people influence their emotions, when they have them, and how they experience or express them (Gross, 1998, 2015). In marriage, regulation matters because one partner's emotional expression becomes part of the other partner's environment. Regulation is not the absence of emotion. It is the ability to let emotion inform behavior without letting it take over the relationship.

CORE TEACHING

Under pressure, thoughts can become fast, automatic, and convincing. Cognitive therapy has long emphasized the connection between automatic interpretations, emotion, and behavior (Beck et al., 1979). A partner may think, 'They do not care,' when the observable behavior is that the partner is quiet. Another may think, 'I have to handle everything,' when they have not clearly asked for help. The thought may feel like fact because it is attached to strong emotion.

Acceptance and Commitment Therapy offers a useful question for couples: What valued action can I take while this difficult feeling is present? Psychological flexibility involves contacting the present moment and choosing behavior guided by values even when difficult thoughts and feelings are present (Hayes et al., 2012). In marriage, this means a partner can be angry and still choose not to insult, afraid and still choose not to control, overwhelmed and still choose not to disappear without explanation.

Emotional regulation protects the relationship process. It allows partners to pause before contempt, name fear beneath anger, ask for time before shutdown, and return after a break. Regulation does not solve every issue, but it creates the conditions under which issues can be discussed with less harm.

GUIDED EXERCISE

MY REGULATION SIGNALS

Identify the signs that tell you your body and mind are becoming activated.

Reflection Prompt	Response / Notes
When I am becoming emotionally activated, my body usually shows it through:	
When I am becoming emotionally activated, my thoughts usually sound like:	
When I am becoming emotionally activated, my tone or behavior may become:	
The emotion underneath my reaction is often:	
The value I want to act from instead is:	
A phrase I can use to slow myself down is:	
A regulation practice I can use before continuing is:	

PAUSE AND RETURN AGREEMENT

A pause is protective only when it is named, time-limited, and followed by return.

Reflection Prompt	Response / Notes
When one of us needs a pause, we will say:	
A healthy pause should usually last:	
During the pause, each partner will:	
During the pause, each partner will not:	
The person who asked for the pause will return by:	
If the conversation still feels unsafe after the pause, we will:	
Our shared reminder that a pause is not abandonment is:	

VALUES-BASED RESPONSE PRACTICE

Use this when you feel the urge to react from activation.

Reflection Prompt	Response / Notes
The feeling present right now is:	
The urge this feeling creates is:	
The story my mind is telling me is:	
The value I want to honor is:	
The response that moves us toward that value is:	
The response that would move us away from that value is:	
The small action I choose is:	

ACT SKILL

PSYCHOLOGICAL FLEXIBILITY UNDER PRESSURE

ACT adds a useful layer to emotional regulation because it does not require partners to eliminate difficult feelings before acting well. The goal is psychological flexibility: noticing what is happening in the present moment, making room for difficult internal experiences, reconnecting with values, and choosing committed action even when stress is still present (Hayes et al., 2012). For couples, this matters because pressure often creates automatic reactions. A partner may feel afraid and move toward control, ashamed and move toward defensiveness, hurt and move toward contempt, or overwhelmed and move toward disappearance. ACT-informed practice helps the partner slow that movement enough to ask, 'What is this feeling pulling me to do, and what would my values ask me to do instead?'

These ACT components should not be used to minimize harm or ask one partner to accept unsafe behavior. Acceptance does not mean approval. It means acknowledging the presence of a feeling, thought, memory, or bodily response without letting it become the sole driver of behavior. A person can accept that fear is present while still refusing to threaten, control, or withdraw punitively. A person can accept that hurt is present while still choosing language that protects dignity.

GUIDED EXERCISE

DEFUSING FROM STRESS STORIES

Defusion means creating enough distance from a thought to see it as a thought, not as the whole truth. Under pressure, partners often fuse with stress stories such as 'I am alone,' 'They do not care,' 'I have to fix this myself,' or 'Nothing will change.' These stories may contain pain or partial truth, but when treated as complete fact, they can drive reactions that make the relationship less safe.

Reflection Prompt	Response / Notes
A stress story my mind tells me under pressure is:	
When I believe this story completely, I tend to react by:	
The emotion underneath this story is often:	
The need underneath this story may be:	
A defusion phrase I can practice is: "I am having the thought that..."	
A more balanced statement I can try is:	
One question I can ask before reacting from this story is:	

GUIDED EXERCISE

THE PRESSURE CHOICE POINT

A choice point is the moment when pressure pulls a partner toward an away move or a toward move. Away moves are behaviors that move the relationship away from safety, connection, repair, or shared values. Toward moves are behaviors that move the relationship toward dignity, clarity, support, accountability, and repair. The goal is not to feel perfectly calm. The goal is to notice the pull and choose the next action more consciously.

Reflection Prompt	Response / Notes
The pressure situation we are working with is:	
The difficult thoughts that show up are:	
The difficult feelings that show up are:	
The away move I am pulled toward is:	
The cost of that away move is:	
The relationship value I want to return to is:	
A toward move I can practice instead is:	
A phrase that can help me pause at the choice point is:	

GUIDED EXERCISE

WILLINGNESS WITHOUT PERMISSION FOR HARM

Willingness means making room for discomfort that comes with doing what matters. In relationships, this may mean being willing to feel vulnerable while asking for support, willing to feel embarrassed while apologizing, willing to feel anxious while allowing a partner space to regulate, or willing to feel uncertainty while making the next responsible decision. Willingness is not permission for harm. It is the ability to stay connected to values while discomfort is present.

Reflection Prompt	Response / Notes
A feeling I usually try to avoid during shared stress is:	
The behavior I use to avoid this feeling is:	
How that avoidance affects my partner or the relationship is:	
What I may need to be willing to feel in order to act with more care is:	
A boundary that must remain protected while I practice willingness is:	
A values-based action I can take while this feeling is present is:	

COMMITTED ACTION UNDER PRESSURE

Committed action is the small, concrete behavior that expresses a value. For couples, the action should be specific enough to practice this week. A value such as support may become the action of checking in at 7 p.m. A value such as respect may become the action of taking a pause before raising a voice. A value such as accountability may become the action of returning to repair without making excuses. Resilience grows when values become repeatable behavior.

Reflection Prompt	Response / Notes
The relationship value I want to practice this week is:	
The pressure that may make this value difficult to practice is:	
The difficult thought or feeling I expect to show up is:	
The committed action I will take anyway is:	
When and where I will practice this action is:	
How my partner will know I am practicing it is:	
How I will repair if I miss the action is:	

COUPLE PRACTICE

SHARED VALUES UNDER PRESSURE

Partners do not have to experience the stressor the same way in order to share values. During a shared stressor, values function as a compass. They help the couple decide how they want to behave when emotions are high, resources are low, and certainty is limited.

Couple Prompt	Response / Notes
The value we most want our relationship to reflect during this stressor is:	
This value would look like the following behavior from Partner One:	
This value would look like the following behavior from Partner Two:	
An away move that pulls us from this value is:	
A toward move that returns us to this value is:	
Our shared ACT phrase during pressure will be:	
We will revisit this practice on:	

CHAPTER 9

COMMUNICATION UNDER PRESSURE

Communication is often presented as the solution to relationship distress, but communication under pressure is more complicated than simply talking more. Some couples talk for hours and never reach the real issue. Others avoid conflict so effectively that the relationship appears calm while resentment grows underneath. The problem is not always the absence of words. Sometimes the problem is timing, tone, listening, emotional readiness, or the meaning partners assign to each other's words.

Communication under stress is shaped by appraisal. People respond not only to what is said, but to what they believe the words mean and whether they feel resourced enough to respond (Lazarus & Folkman, 1984). Under shared stress, partners are more likely to listen for threat. A question may sound like criticism. Silence may feel like abandonment. A practical suggestion may feel like control.

CORE TEACHING

The distinction between content and process is essential. Content is what the couple is talking about. Process is how the couple treats each other while talking about it. Research on marital interaction has shown that conflict processes, affect, and repair patterns matter for long-term relationship outcomes (Gottman & Levenson, 1992, 2000). A couple may solve the bill, the schedule, or the decision while injuring the relationship through contempt, criticism, defensiveness, or withdrawal.

Healthy communication under pressure keeps concerns as specific as possible. Instead of 'You never support me,' a partner might say, 'When I handled the appointment alone after telling you I was overwhelmed, I felt unsupported.' Instead of 'You are controlling,' a partner might say, 'When decisions are made before we talk, I feel like my voice does not matter.' Specific language gives the relationship a better chance to respond.

GUIDED EXERCISE

COMMUNICATION VALUES

Define the values that should guide communication when pressure rises.

Reflection Prompt	Response / Notes
When we communicate under pressure, we want our relationship to reflect:	
Respect means:	
Honesty means:	
Emotional safety means:	
Accountability means:	
Support means:	
Repair means:	
The kind of communication we want to practice during stress is:	

TIMING AGREEMENT

Decide when difficult conversations should and should not happen.

Reflection Prompt	Response / Notes
Difficult conversations are most productive for us when:	
Difficult conversations are least productive for us when:	
We agree not to begin major conversations when:	
If a topic is important but the timing is poor, we will say:	
The time we will return to the conversation is:	
Topics that require scheduled conversation include:	
Topics that can be handled briefly include:	

SPEAKING AND LISTENING AGREEMENT

Use specific language and slow defensiveness.

Reflection Prompt	Response / Notes
When raising a concern, we will name the specific behavior or situation:	
The impact was:	
The need is:	
The request is:	
Before responding defensively, we will ask:	
When we do not understand, we will ask:	
When we feel accused, we will say:	
When we need to reset, we will say:	

CONFLICT BOUNDARIES

Name behaviors that remain outside emotional safety even under stress.

Reflection Prompt	Response / Notes
During conflict, we agree not to use name calling:	
Threats:	
Mocking or contempt:	
Bringing up old wounds to win:	
Using children as messengers:	
Financial intimidation:	
Physical intimidation:	
Public humiliation:	
Silence as punishment:	
If one of these boundaries is crossed, we will:	

PART FOUR

ROLES, REPAIR, AND RECONNECTION

CHAPTER 10

ROLE ADJUSTMENT AND INVISIBLE LABOR

Shared stressors do not only affect how couples feel. They affect what couples must do. Someone has to make the calls, manage the appointments, review the budget, comfort the child, update the family, organize the paperwork, remember the deadlines, and absorb the emotional tone of the household. Under pressure, love becomes practical very quickly.

Role adjustment is central to marital resilience because a relationship can have strong affection and still become strained when roles no longer fit the conditions of life. Family systems theory reminds us that roles and structures shape how the family system operates under strain (Minuchin, 1974). When the system changes but roles do not, one partner may begin carrying more silently until resentment becomes the relationship's emotional language.

CORE TEACHING

Resentment often grows in the space between contribution and recognition. A partner may not resent carrying more for a season. They may resent carrying more without acknowledgment, without agreement, without relief, and without any sign that the imbalance will be revisited. In this way, resentment is often information. It may signal an unspoken need, an unfair pattern, a lack of appreciation, or a role that has expanded beyond capacity.

Invisible labor includes remembering, anticipating, organizing, monitoring, planning, emotionally preparing, and holding responsibility before any task is visible. Under pressure, invisible labor often expands dramatically. A partner who says, 'Just tell me what to do,' may believe they are cooperating. The other partner may hear, 'You remain the manager, and I will be the assistant.' Role adjustment requires not only assistance but ownership.

GUIDED EXERCISE

CURRENT ROLE INVENTORY

Make the current distribution of responsibilities visible.

Reflection Prompt	Response / Notes
Partner One currently carries responsibility for household tasks:	
Partner One currently carries responsibility for financial management:	
Partner One currently carries responsibility for childcare, parenting, or caregiving:	
Partner One currently carries responsibility for appointments and scheduling:	
Partner One currently carries responsibility for emotional support or conflict repair:	
Partner Two currently carries responsibility for household tasks:	
Partner Two currently carries responsibility for financial management:	
Partner Two currently carries responsibility for childcare, parenting, or caregiving:	
Partner Two currently carries responsibility for appointments and scheduling:	
Partner Two currently carries responsibility for emotional support or conflict repair:	

INVISIBLE LABOR

Make remembering, anticipating, organizing, and emotional preparation visible.

Reflection Prompt	Response / Notes
The invisible labor Partner One carries includes:	
The invisible labor Partner Two carries includes:	
The invisible labor that feels most overlooked is:	
The invisible labor that needs to be shared is:	
The invisible labor that needs appreciation is:	
One part of the mental load that needs ownership instead of assistance is:	

REBALANCING PLAN

Clarify what will continue, shift, simplify, or receive outside support.

Reflection Prompt	Response / Notes
One responsibility Partner One can continue carrying is:	
One responsibility Partner Two can continue carrying is:	
One responsibility Partner One needs help with is:	
One responsibility Partner Two needs help with is:	
One responsibility that should shift temporarily is:	
One responsibility that should shift permanently is:	
One task that can be postponed is:	
One task that can be simplified is:	
One task that can be delegated is:	
One outside resource we can use is:	

LOAD AWARENESS CHECKPOINT

Role adjustment works best when the couple notices overload before resentment becomes the main signal. A load awareness checkpoint helps partners ask whether one person is carrying too much because of temporary necessity, quiet obligation, or an outdated role pattern.

Reflection Prompt	Response / Notes
The responsibility most likely to overload Partner One is:	
The early sign Partner One is becoming overloaded is:	
The responsibility most likely to overload Partner Two is:	
The early sign Partner Two is becoming overloaded is:	
The responsibility we can shift before overload becomes resentment is:	
The responsibility that requires outside support is:	

APPRECIATION AND RECOGNITION

Acknowledgment does not replace change, but it opens the door to repair and rebalancing.

Reflection Prompt	Response / Notes
One thing Partner One has been carrying that deserves acknowledgment is:	
One thing Partner Two has been carrying that deserves acknowledgment is:	
Partner One wants to say to Partner Two:	
Partner Two wants to say to Partner One:	
A contribution we do not want to overlook again is:	
We will review this role arrangement on:	

CHAPTER 11

REPAIR, FORGIVENESS, AND FOLLOW THROUGH

No couple communicates perfectly under pressure. Partners will speak too sharply, withdraw too long, misread each other, become defensive, offer the wrong support, or avoid a difficult topic until resentment leaks out. The question is not whether rupture will ever happen. The question is whether the relationship has a path back.

Repair is not simply saying, 'I am sorry.' Repair is the disciplined return to responsibility after harm. It includes acknowledging what happened, listening to impact, clarifying intention without using it as a defense, taking ownership, changing behavior, and reconnecting in a way that respects the injured partner's pace. Forgiveness may become part of this process, especially when support was needed but not received, but forgiveness should never be used to bypass accountability or rush a partner out of pain.

CORE TEACHING

A weak apology often centers the speaker's discomfort. It says, 'I am sorry you feel that way,' or 'I already said I was sorry,' or 'I was just stressed.' A meaningful apology names the behavior and impact. It might say, 'I was overwhelmed, but I still need to take responsibility for how I spoke to you. The pressure explains my reaction, but it does not excuse the impact.' This kind of apology keeps context and accountability together.

Forgiveness may be part of repair, but it cannot be demanded. Forgiveness in couples is most meaningful when connected to accountability, changed behavior, and genuine healing rather than pressure to move on quickly (Aalgaard et al., 2016). Repair should not be used to rush pain out of the room. It should create conditions where trust can gradually become believable again.

GUIDED EXERCISE

PAUSE BEFORE REPAIR

Before beginning repair, confirm that the conversation can happen with enough safety and regulation.

Reflection Prompt	Response / Notes
Am I regulated enough to listen?	
Am I willing to understand impact, not only defend intention?	
Am I willing to take responsibility for my part?	
Am I safe to speak honestly?	
Is this conversation safe to have without professional support?	
If the answer is no, what needs to happen before repair can begin?	

NAMING THE RUPTURE

Name what happened before trying to move past it.

Reflection Prompt	Response / Notes
The rupture happened when:	
The topic was:	
The behavior that caused hurt was:	
The emotional impact was:	
The relational impact was:	
The old wound or pattern this may have activated was:	
The part that still feels unresolved is:	

RESPONSIBILITY AND IMPACT STATEMENTS

The partner repairing should answer the first prompts. The partner receiving repair should answer the impact prompts.

Reflection Prompt	Response / Notes
What I did or said was:	
What I intended was:	
What I understand the impact may have been is:	
What I need to take responsibility for is:	
What I should not excuse by blaming stress is:	
What I want to do differently next time is:	
When this happened, I felt:	
The meaning I made of it was:	
What would help repair feel believable is:	
The behavior I need to see change is:	

FOLLOW THROUGH

Repair becomes believable through changed behavior.

Reflection Prompt	Response / Notes
The specific behavior that needs to change is:	
The specific action that will show change is:	
The time frame for follow through is:	
How we will discuss progress is:	
What we will do if the pattern repeats is:	
When professional support may be needed:	

FORGIVENESS AFTER MISSED SUPPORT

There will be times when support is needed but not received. A partner may miss the cue, offer the wrong kind of help, become too depleted to respond well, or fail to understand the importance of the moment until later. Forgiveness can be part of the repair plan, but it should be paced, honest, and connected to accountability. In couples, forgiveness is most helpful when it supports healing rather than pressure to move on without change (Aalgaard et al., 2016).

Forgiveness does not mean pretending the support gap did not hurt. It does not mean abandoning boundaries or accepting repeated neglect. It means the couple creates a responsible way to acknowledge what was missed, repair what can be repaired, and decide what must change so the same injury is less likely to repeat.

Reflection Prompt	Response / Notes
The moment when support was needed but not received was:	
What I needed then was:	
What was missing or misaligned was:	
The meaning I made of the missed support was:	
What I need acknowledged before forgiveness can become possible is:	
The accountability or changed behavior I need to see is:	
What I am willing to release, if repair is sincere, is:	
What I am not ready to release yet is:	
The boundary or support I need while forgiveness develops is:	

FORGIVENESS WITH ACCOUNTABILITY STATEMENT

Use this statement only when it feels honest and safe. Forgiveness should not be performed to avoid conflict or to protect the other partner from discomfort.

Reflection Prompt	Response / Notes
I am willing to work toward forgiveness when:	
Forgiveness will require the following repair:	
Forgiveness will require the following follow-through:	
Forgiveness does not mean I am agreeing to:	
The next conversation we need to have is:	

CHAPTER 12

RECONNECTION, PLEASANTRIES, AND POSITIVE EMOTIONAL PRESENCE

Repair addresses injury. Reconnection restores relational warmth. The two are related, but they are not identical. A couple may apologize and still feel distant. A partner may understand what went wrong and still not feel ready for closeness. Reconnection should not be forced, especially after serious rupture. It should respect pace, safety, and the seriousness of what happened.

Under pressure, couples can become so focused on solving problems that the relationship becomes only a crisis management unit. Positive emotional presence helps remind the couple that the relationship is more than the stressor. Research on positive emotional connection in long-term couples suggests that shared positive emotion can have meaningful relational and health implications (Wells et al., 2022).

CORE TEACHING

Reconnection does not mean pretending the conflict never happened. It means creating a humane path back after accountability has begun. Sometimes reconnection is physical affection. Sometimes it is a shared walk, a quiet meal, a prayer, a brief moment of humor, a statement of appreciation, or sitting in the same room without solving anything. The form should fit the rupture and the readiness of both partners.

Positive emotional presence is not forced positivity. It is the deliberate protection of warmth, dignity, and humanity while pressure remains real. A couple may still be facing financial strain, illness, grief, or uncertainty, but it can choose small acts that keep the stressor from occupying every emotional room in the relationship.

GUIDED EXERCISE

RECONNECTION READINESS

Use this before attempting reconnection after conflict or strain.

Reflection Prompt	Response / Notes
The rupture or stressful moment we are recovering from is:	
What still needs repair before reconnection can feel genuine is:	
What feels safe to offer right now is:	
What does not feel safe or appropriate yet is:	
Physical affection feels appropriate when:	
Physical affection does not feel appropriate when:	
A calming shared activity we can do after repair is:	

POSITIVE PRESENCE INVENTORY

Identify small practices that restore warmth without denying pressure.

Reflection Prompt	Response / Notes
A small act of affection that helps me feel connected is:	
A small act of appreciation that helps me feel seen is:	
A shared routine that helps us feel like partners is:	
A conversation topic that helps us be more than the stressor is:	
A quiet form of presence that helps is:	
A form of humor, memory, or tenderness that still feels available is:	
One reconnection practice we can repeat this week is:	

EVERYDAY PLEASANTRIES AND APPRECIATION PRACTICE

Long-term couples can begin to treat support as obligation rather than care. The partner who helps with the task, carries the load, listens, adjusts, or shows up may stop hearing simple words such as 'thank you,' 'I appreciate you,' or 'that helped me.' These pleasantries are not shallow manners. They are small acts of recognition that keep support visible. Positive emotional connection in long-term couples has meaningful relational implications, especially when warmth remains present in ordinary interaction (Wells et al., 2022).

Appreciation should be specific and sincere. It should not be used to avoid a needed role adjustment or to cover over harm. A good 'thank you' names the action and the meaning: 'Thank you for taking that call when I was overwhelmed. It helped me feel less alone.'

Reflection Prompt	Response / Notes
One support action my partner often provides that I may take for granted is:	
One simple pleasantry my partner deserves to hear more often is:	
A specific thank you I can offer this week is:	
A contribution I want to notice before it becomes invisible is:	
The time of day or situation when I can practice appreciation is:	
When I receive appreciation, it helps me feel:	
Appreciation should not be used to avoid discussing:	
One appreciation ritual we can practice during shared stress is:	

THE THANK-YOU RULE DURING SHARED STRESS

When one partner temporarily carries more of the load, the other partner should not treat that support as automatic. A simple thank you does not erase the need for rebalancing, but it protects the supporting partner from feeling invisible.

Reflection Prompt	Response / Notes
When Partner One carries extra weight, Partner Two will acknowledge it by saying:	

Reflection Prompt	Response / Notes
When Partner Two carries extra weight, Partner One will acknowledge it by saying:	
The kind of appreciation that feels sincere to Partner One is:	
The kind of appreciation that feels sincere to Partner Two is:	
We will avoid using appreciation as a substitute for:	

RECONNECTION AGREEMENT

Create a realistic ritual of reconnection for the current season.

Reflection Prompt	Response / Notes
Our reconnection practice will be:	
We will practice it when:	
We will not use reconnection to avoid:	
We will respect pace by:	
We will check whether it is helping by asking:	
A follow-up check in should happen on:	

PART FIVE

CRISIS PLANNING AND RESILIENCE

CHAPTER 13

CREATING THE SHARED STRESSOR CRISIS PLAN

A crisis plan may sound too practical for love, but strategic love is not cold. It is intentional. It recognizes that under shared pressure, affection alone may not be enough to guide communication, support, role adjustment, repair, and help seeking. A plan does not remove tenderness from love. It gives tenderness a pathway to remain available when fear, fatigue, and uncertainty make tenderness harder to access.

The Shared Stressor Crisis Plan brings together the central practices of this workbook: naming the stressor, understanding each partner's experience, identifying resource depletion, clarifying support, coordinating coping, creating communication agreements, adjusting roles, establishing emotional safety boundaries, planning repair, identifying outside support, and reviewing the crisis after the pressure decreases. This structure aligns with the broader understanding that resilience depends on adaptation, meaning making, communication, flexibility, and access to resources (Walsh, 2016).

CORE TEACHING

The crisis plan is not a guarantee that conflict will disappear. It is a structure that helps the couple avoid entering every difficult season as if they have learned nothing from the last one. It gives the relationship a process when instinct is unreliable. It also helps the couple identify when the stressor exceeds what the relationship can handle privately.

The plan should be completed during a calm or semi-calm time whenever possible. If the couple is already in active crisis, move more slowly. Begin with the most urgent sections: safety, resource depletion, support needs, communication boundaries, and outside help. A plan should never be used to pressure a partner into unsafe conversation. Where fear, coercion, violence, or retaliation are present, the priority is safety and qualified support.

STEP ONE: NAME THE SHARED STRESSOR

Name the pressure clearly so the couple can identify what is acting on the relationship.

Reflection Prompt	Response / Notes
The shared stressor we are facing is:	
What makes this stressor shared is:	
This stressor is affecting our relationship by changing:	
This stressor is affecting our daily life by changing:	
The parts of this stressor we can influence are:	
The parts of this stressor we cannot fully control are:	

STEP TWO: IDENTIFY HOW EACH PARTNER IS AFFECTED

A shared stressor does not mean both partners experience the stressor in the same way.

Reflection Prompt	Response / Notes
Partner One: Emotionally, this stressor affects me by:	
Partner One: Mentally, this stressor affects me by:	
Partner One: Physically, this stressor affects me by:	
Partner One: Practically, this stressor affects me by:	

Reflection Prompt	Response / Notes
Partner Two: Emotionally, this stressor affects me by:	
Partner Two: Mentally, this stressor affects me by:	
Partner Two: Physically, this stressor affects me by:	
Partner Two: Practically, this stressor affects me by:	
Together, we notice that our experiences are similar in these ways:	
Together, we notice that our experiences are different in these ways:	

STEP THREE: IDENTIFY RESOURCE DEPLETION

Identify what is being drained before depletion becomes blame.

Reflection Prompt	Response / Notes
The resources most depleted right now are:	
The resources most threatened right now are:	
The resources we need to protect immediately are:	
The resources we need to restore over time are:	

Reflection Prompt	Response / Notes
The resource each partner most needs right now is:	
One small action that could protect or restore a resource this week is:	
One demand we may need to reduce, postpone, delegate, or simplify is:	

STEP FOUR: DEFINE SUPPORT CLEARLY

Support must be clarified, not assumed.

Reflection Prompt	Response / Notes
Partner One: When I am under pressure, support looks like:	
Partner One: The kind of support that helps me most is:	
Partner One: The kind of support that does not help me is:	
Partner Two: When I am under pressure, support looks like:	
Partner Two: The kind of support that helps me most is:	
Partner Two: The kind of support that does not help me is:	
Together, we agree to ask this question before assuming what support is needed:	

STEP FOUR-A: NOTICE DISTRESS AND LIGHTEN THE LOAD EARLY

Support becomes stronger when the couple notices distress before distress becomes blame. Early awareness allows partners to reduce load, offer support, or seek help before one partner becomes overwhelmed.

Reflection Prompt	Response / Notes
Partner One early distress cues are:	
Partner Two early distress cues are:	
When we notice distress, our first question will be:	
One way we can lighten the load without taking over is:	
One responsibility we can temporarily shift when distress is high is:	
One sign that outside support may be needed is:	

STEP FIVE: IDENTIFY DEFAULT COPING STYLES

Make coping styles understandable and accountable.

Reflection Prompt	Response / Notes
Partner One: When I am under pressure, I tend to cope by:	
Partner One: This helps me because:	
Partner One: This may affect you by:	
Partner One: What I am willing to adjust for the sake of the relationship is:	

Reflection Prompt	Response / Notes
Partner Two: When I am under pressure, I tend to cope by:	
Partner Two: This helps me because:	
Partner Two: This may affect you by:	
Partner Two: What I am willing to adjust for the sake of the relationship is:	
Together, we agree that when our coping styles collide, we will:	

STEP FIVE-A: CREATE A BIDIRECTIONAL LOAD-SHARING PLAN

When both partners face the same stressor, the load may need to move back and forth. Sometimes Partner One carries more while Partner Two stabilizes. At other times, Partner Two carries more while Partner One stabilizes. The goal is not perfect equality in every moment. The goal is conscious, temporary, appreciated, and revisited support.

Reflection Prompt	Response / Notes
When Partner One has lower capacity, Partner Two can carry:	
When Partner Two has lower capacity, Partner One can carry:	
The support we need while one partner stabilizes is:	
How we will signal that capacity is changing:	
How we will prevent temporary imbalance from becoming permanent obligation:	
The date or condition when we will revisit this plan is:	

STEP FIVE-B: CREATE AN ACT-BASED CHOICE POINT PLAN

Use this step to decide how the couple will respond when difficult thoughts and feelings appear during pressure. The goal is not to remove distress before acting. The goal is to notice distress, return to values, and choose a committed action that protects the relationship (Hayes et al., 2012).

Reflection Prompt	Response / Notes
The difficult thought or stress story most likely to take over is:	
When this thought takes over, our common away move is:	
The relationship value we want to return to is:	
The feeling we may need to make room for without acting harmfully is:	
The toward move we will practice is:	
The committed action we will take this week is:	
The ACT phrase we will use to slow the moment is:	

STEP SIX: CREATE A PRESSURE COMMUNICATION AGREEMENT

Stress can make people more reactive, defensive, withdrawn, or threat sensitive.

Reflection Prompt	Response / Notes
When one of us feels over-whelmed, we will signal it by saying:	
When one of us needs a pause, we agree that the pause will last:	
When the pause ends, we will return by:	

Reflection Prompt	Response / Notes
Topics we should not discuss when exhausted, hungry, flooded, or distracted include:	
The best time for difficult conversations is usually:	
During pressure, we agree not to use the following behaviors:	
Our regular check in schedule during this stressful season will be:	

STEP SEVEN: ADJUST ROLES AND RESPONSIBILITIES

Some role changes are necessary, but they should not remain invisible.

Reflection Prompt	Response / Notes
Responsibilities that have increased because of this stressor include:	
Responsibilities Partner One is currently carrying include:	
Responsibilities Partner Two is currently carrying include:	
Responsibilities that feel invisible or underacknowledged include:	
Responsibilities that need to shift temporarily include:	
Responsibilities that can be postponed, simplified, delegated, or removed include:	
One area Partner One can take ownership of is:	

Reflection Prompt	Response / Notes
One area Partner Two can take ownership of is:	
The plan to revisit this role arrangement is:	

STEP SEVEN-A: APPRECIATION AND PLEASANTRY PRACTICE

When responsibilities shift, appreciation helps keep labor visible. Simple pleasantries protect the relationship from treating support as obligation.

Reflection Prompt	Response / Notes
The support action we agree to acknowledge more often is:	
The phrase we will use to thank each other during this stressful season is:	
The contribution we do not want to overlook again is:	
How we will express appreciation without avoiding needed rebalancing:	

STEP EIGHT: ESTABLISH EMOTIONAL SAFETY BOUNDARIES

Pressure does not excuse harm.

Reflection Prompt	Response / Notes
During stress, we agree that the following behaviors are not acceptable:	
If one of these boundaries is crossed, we agree to:	

Reflection Prompt	Response / Notes
When a conversation becomes unsafe, we will:	
When one partner feels afraid, intimidated, or emotionally unsafe, the next step will be:	
Professional or outside support may be needed if:	
This relationship remains a safe place for honesty when we both commit to:	

STEP NINE: CREATE A REPAIR PLAN

Repair requires acknowledgment, ownership, impact, changed behavior, and follow through.

Reflection Prompt	Response / Notes
When I hurt you under pressure, I want to practice repairing by saying:	
When you hurt me under pressure, what helps repair is:	
A meaningful apology in our relationship includes:	
A weak or incomplete apology sounds like:	
When we need to repair after conflict, we will ask:	
The behavior that most needs to change after repair is:	

Reflection Prompt	Response / Notes
The follow through that would make repair believable is:	
A reconnection practice we can use after repair is:	

STEP NINE-A: INCLUDE FORGIVENESS AFTER MISSED SUPPORT

Because support will sometimes be missed or misaligned, the crisis plan should include a way to work toward forgiveness without bypassing accountability.

Reflection Prompt	Response / Notes
When support is missed, we agree to name:	
The apology or acknowledgment that helps repair missed support is:	
The follow-through that makes forgiveness more believable is:	
The boundary that must remain in place while forgiveness develops is:	
The phrase we can use when we are not ready to forgive yet is:	

STEP TEN: IDENTIFY OUTSIDE SUPPORT

Some stressors exceed the internal resources of the couple.

Reflection Prompt	Response / Notes
Signs that we need outside support include:	
The kind of outside support that may help us is:	
People or professionals we can contact include:	
Support we are willing to accept includes:	
Support we are hesitant to accept and why:	
If safety becomes a concern, the steps we will take are:	

CHAPTER 14

POST-CRISIS REVIEW AND RELATIONSHIP LEARNING

After pressure decreases, many couples want to move on quickly. The desire is understandable. Crisis is exhausting, and normal life can feel like relief. But if the couple moves on without reflection, the relationship may carry unprocessed injuries, unrevised roles, and unexamined support failures into the next season.

A relationship under pressure must learn in real time and after the pressure passes. Senge's work on learning organizations emphasizes that adaptive systems examine patterns, mental models, shared vision, and team learning (Senge, 1990). A marriage is not a business, but it can still learn from its own patterns. Post-crisis review turns hardship into information without romanticizing the hardship itself.

CORE TEACHING

Post-crisis review should not be a trial. It is not a place to prove who failed. It is a place to ask what happened between the partners, what helped, what hurt, what needs repair, what resources were depleted, and what the couple should change before the next stressful season. Family resilience research emphasizes the importance of communication, flexible organization, shared meaning, and resource use in adaptation after adversity (Walsh, 2016).

Learning requires both honesty and compassion. If the review becomes blame, partners will defend. If it becomes avoidance, nothing changes. The goal is to examine the system with enough care that both partners can remain engaged.

GUIDED EXERCISE

POST-CRISIS REVIEW

Use this exercise after the pressure decreases enough for reflection.

Reflection Prompt	Response / Notes
The stressor affected us most strongly by:	
What we handled well was:	

Reflection Prompt	Response / Notes
Where we struggled was:	
The support that helped most was:	
The support that was missing or misaligned was:	
The resource that became most depleted was:	
The role adjustment that worked was:	
The role adjustment that needs to change is:	
The communication pattern we want to keep is:	
The communication pattern we do not want to repeat is:	
The repair still needed is:	

WHAT WE LEARNED

Use this section to turn experience into relational learning.

Reflection Prompt	Response / Notes
What I learned about myself is:	
What I learned about my partner is:	
What I learned about our coping pattern is:	

Reflection Prompt	Response / Notes
What I learned about our support system is:	
What I learned about our emotional safety needs is:	
What I learned about the outside support we need is:	
What we will change in our crisis plan before the next stressful season is:	

RELATIONSHIP LEARNING AGREEMENT

Identify one change that will become part of the relationship's future operating system.

Reflection Prompt	Response / Notes
One pattern we will keep is:	
One pattern we will interrupt earlier is:	
One agreement we will revise is:	
One support practice we will continue is:	
One role arrangement we will revisit is:	
One outside resource we will keep available is:	
We will review these changes on:	

CHAPTER 15

WHEN OUTSIDE SUPPORT IS NEEDED

Some stressors exceed the internal resources of the couple. This does not mean the relationship has failed. It means the couple is willing to be honest about limits. A spouse can be deeply loving and still not be equipped to provide therapy, medical care, legal guidance, financial planning, crisis intervention, or specialized caregiving support.

A resilient system does not prove its strength by refusing support. Family resilience research emphasizes that resilience is strengthened not only by internal family processes but also by relational and community resources (Walsh, 2016). Outside support may become necessary when the stressor is too complex, too painful, too dangerous, or too persistent for the couple to manage alone.

CORE TEACHING

Couples therapy or counseling may help when the same conflict repeats without resolution, communication regularly escalates into blame or shutdown, trust has been damaged, role imbalance has become a source of resentment, or the couple needs help creating a safe process. Individual therapy may be appropriate when one partner is experiencing anxiety, depression, trauma symptoms, grief, panic, emotional numbness, chronic overwhelm, difficulty regulating conflict, or difficulty asking for or receiving support.

Medical or psychiatric support may be needed when stress affects sleep, appetite, concentration, functioning, physical health, mood, substance use, panic, severe depression, suicidal thoughts, or major changes in behavior. Financial, legal, caregiving, or community support may be needed when the stressor involves debt, job loss, business instability, estate concerns, custody, immigration, housing, caregiving, respite care, or specialized practical needs.

Safety support is needed when pressure becomes danger. Physical violence, threats of harm, coercive control, intimidation, fear of retaliation, forced isolation, financial control used to trap or punish, sexual coercion, stalking, destruction of property, and repeated humiliation are not ordinary communication problems. In these situations, the priority is safety, not relational repair.

GUIDED EXERCISE

DO WE NEED OUTSIDE SUPPORT?

Use these questions to determine whether the couple needs help beyond the relationship.

Reflection Prompt	Response / Notes
Are we repeating the same conflict without meaningful change?	
Do one or both of us feel emotionally unsafe during difficult conversations?	
Have apologies stopped leading to changed behavior?	
Is resentment becoming the main emotional language of the relationship?	
Are we avoiding important topics because we are afraid of what will happen?	
Are children or other family members being affected by our conflict?	
Are we relying on one partner to carry too much?	
Are we facing a stressor that requires professional knowledge?	
Are we isolated from support?	
Is either partner afraid?	
Do we need help creating a safe process?	

PROFESSIONAL SUPPORT PLANNING

Create a first step toward appropriate support.

Reflection Prompt	Response / Notes
The kind of support we may need is:	
The concern we need help with is:	
A professional or resource we can contact is:	
The barrier that makes it hard to seek help is:	
The first step we can take is:	
The person responsible for taking that first step is:	
The date we will take that step is:	

SAFETY REFLECTION

Complete this section only if it is safe to do so. If safety is a concern, seek qualified support before engaging relational repair exercises.

Reflection Prompt	Response / Notes
The behaviors that would make ordinary communication tools unsafe are:	
The person, professional, or service I can contact if safety becomes a concern is:	
A safe place or support option available to me is:	
A first step toward safety, clarity, or protection is:	
What I need to remember about the difference between pressure and danger is:	

CLOSING REFLECTION

Seeking help does not mean the relationship has failed. It means the couple is willing to be honest about the limits of private effort. A resilient relationship does not prove its strength by refusing support. It proves its maturity by knowing when support is needed and by taking the next responsible step toward safety, healing, and clarity.

CLOSING NOTE

THE SMALL STEPS THAT KEEP LOVE ALIVE

Love under pressure is not measured only by what a couple feels in the easiest seasons. It is revealed when life becomes heavy, when both partners are tired, when certainty is limited, and when the relationship must decide whether pressure will turn two people against each other or call them into a deeper form of responsibility.

The purpose of this workbook has not been to romanticize hardship. Pressure is not automatically meaningful. Some seasons are painful simply because they are painful. Some stressors take more than they give. Some relationships reveal patterns under pressure that require serious intervention, boundaries, or endings. Resilience should never be used as a word that asks someone to tolerate harm.

Still, for relationships where both partners are willing to do the work, pressure can become a place of revelation. It shows what has been assumed. It exposes what has been avoided. It reveals whether support is visible, whether roles are sustainable, whether communication protects emotional safety, whether repair is real, and whether the couple has a way to respond when both people are affected at the same time.

Resilience is the choice to show up through intentional actions in the present moment. It is shaped through small steps in the right direction. A couple does not need a grand breakthrough to begin. It can begin by naming the stressor, asking what support looks like, acknowledging invisible labor, using a responsible pause, repairing one injury, or seeking outside support before the system collapses.

The Shared Stressor Crisis Plan is one way to give those small steps structure. It asks couples to prepare before pressure narrows their choices. It gives love a process when instinct is not enough. The plan does not promise that couples will never hurt each other, misunderstand each other, or become overwhelmed. It gives them a way to return when they do.

Love under pressure is not perfect love. It is practiced love. It is love with humility, structure, emotional responsibility, and repair. It is love that understands the storm may come, but the storm does not have to have the final word. The final word can be chosen in small steps, spoken through intentional actions, and lived in the quiet decision to keep showing up with care, truth, and courage while the pressure is real.

RELATIONSHIP RESILIENCE COMMITMENT

Use this commitment as a closing reflection or as the final page of a shared workbook conversation. It is not a promise of perfection. It is a promise to keep practicing intentional care while pressure is real.

Commitment Statement

- ☐ Together, we commit to naming pressure before turning on each other.
- ☐ Together, we commit to clarifying support rather than assuming support.
- ☐ Together, we commit to protecting emotional safety even when emotions are high.
- ☐ Together, we commit to adjusting roles when the old structure no longer fits the present demand.
- ☐ Together, we commit to repairing harm instead of pretending it did not happen.
- ☐ Together, we commit to seeking outside support when our internal resources are not enough.
- ☐ Together, we commit to taking small steps in the right direction while the pressure is real.
- ☐ Together, we commit to noticing distress cues before distress becomes blame.
- ☐ Together, we commit to bidirectional load-sharing when one partner needs temporary stabilization.
- ☐ Together, we commit to using simple pleasantries and specific appreciation so support does not become invisible obligation.
- ☐ Together, we commit to practicing forgiveness with accountability when support is missed or misaligned.
- ☐ Together, we commit to noticing difficult thoughts and feelings without letting them decide how we treat each other.
- ☐ Together, we commit to choosing values-based actions even when pressure makes reactive behavior feel easier.

FINAL REFLECTION

Complete this reflection individually or together.

Reflection Prompt	Response / Notes
The most important thing I learned about myself in this work-book is:	
The most important thing I learned about my partner is:	
The pattern I most want us to change is:	

Reflection Prompt	Response / Notes
The support practice I most want us to continue is:	
The repair practice I most want us to strengthen is:	
The outside support we may need to keep available is:	
The small step in the right direction we will take this week is:	

CHOOSING US UNDER PRESSURE

This agreement is not a promise that we will handle every stressful moment perfectly. It is a reminder of who we are choosing to become while pressure is present. Shared stress can narrow our patience, distort our perception, and pull us into blame, withdrawal, control, or silence. This agreement gives us a place to return when the stressor feels larger than our connection. It reminds us that resilience is not built through perfection, but through presence, shared responsibility, repair, team learning, and small steps in the right direction.

OUR LOVE UNDER PRESSURE AGREEMENT

We, ____ and ______________________________________ __________, enter this agreement with honesty, humility, and intention.

We commit to being present in the current moment, even when the moment is difficult. We understand that pressure may create fear, fatigue, frustration, grief, uncertainty, or emotional depletion, but we agree to keep returning to awareness, care, and responsibility.

We agree to work toward our shared vision for this relationship, our family, and the life we are building together. We recognize that our relationship is a living system. What affects one of us affects both of us. What strengthens one of us can strengthen the relationship. What harms one of us must be addressed with honesty, accountability, and care.

We commit to practicing systems thinking by looking beyond blame and asking what the stressor is doing to our relationship, our roles, our communication, our resources, and our emotional safety. We agree not to make each other the enemy when the true pressure is the stressor we are facing.

We commit to team learning as we move through this stressor. We will listen, adjust, ask better questions, notice what is working, repair what has been injured, and learn from what pressure reveals. We understand that support may need to move in both directions. At times, one of us may need to carry more of the weight while the other stabilizes. At other times, the roles may reverse. We agree to remain aware of each other's distress, to lighten the load where we can, and to return to balance as the stressor subsides.

We commit to facing this stressor together. Our priority is not winning, defending, withdrawing, or proving who has suffered more. Our priority is us: our connection, our survival, our emotional safety, our shared future, and the well-being of our family.

We agree that our love must become visible through action. It will be shown in the way we speak, pause, listen, repair, offer support, express appreciation, share responsibility, and take the next small step. We will remember that simple words still matter. "Thank you." "I see what you are carrying." "I appreciate your support." "I am here." "I choose us." These small acts of acknowledgment help protect love from becoming obligation.

We understand that there may be times when support is needed but not received in the way one of us hoped. When that happens, we agree to seek repair rather than resentment. We will make room for accountability, forgiveness, changed behavior, and renewed effort. Forgiveness does not erase the need for responsibility. Repair does not require perfection. Both require honesty, humility, and the willingness to return to each other with care.

When we need a reminder, we can revisit this agreement. We can return to these words when pressure becomes loud, when one of us feels alone, when the stressor begins to shape our tone, or when we forget that love is practiced in the present moment.

I choose not to handle this alone.
I choose to acknowledge I need spousal support.
I choose to recognize you need spousal support.
I choose to be present.
I choose to listen.
I choose to repair.
I choose to support and receive support.
I choose to notice when my partner is under distress.
I choose to appreciate the help, care, and effort my partner gives.
I choose to face this stressor with my partner, not against my partner.
I choose the work of resilience.
I choose the next small step in the right direction.
I choose us.

COUPLE COMMITMENT

Partner One Name: ______________________________

Signature: ______________________________

Date: ______________________________

Partner Two Name: ______________________________

Signature: ______________________________

Date: ______________________________

Shared Stressor We Are Committing to Face Together: ______________________________

____

____

One Small Step We Will Take This Week: ______________________________

____

____

BIBLIOGRAPHY

Aalgaard, R. A., Bolen, R. M., & Nugent, W. R. (2016). A literature review of forgiveness as a beneficial intervention to increase relationship satisfaction in couples' therapy. Journal of Human Behavior in the Social Environment, 26(1), 46-55. https://doi.org/10.1080/10911359.2015.1059166

Beck, A. T., Rush, A. J., Shaw, B. F., & Emery, G. (1979). Cognitive therapy of depression. Guilford Press.

Bodenmann, G. (2005). Dyadic coping and its significance for marital functioning. In T. A. Revenson, K. Kayser, & G. Bodenmann (Eds.), Couples coping with stress: Emerging perspectives on dyadic coping (pp. 33-49). American Psychological Association. https://doi.org/10.1037/11031-002

Bowlby, J. (1969). Attachment and loss: Vol. 1. Attachment. Basic Books.

Cutrona, C. E. (Ed.). (1996). Social support in couples: Marriage as a resource in times of stress. SAGE.

Falconier, M. K., Jackson, J. B., Hilpert, P., & Bodenmann, G. (2015). Dyadic coping and relationship satisfaction: A meta-analysis. Clinical Psychology Review, 42, 28-46. https://doi.org/10.1016/j.cpr.2015.07.002

Gottman, J. M., & Levenson, R. W. (1992). Marital processes predictive of later dissolution: Behavior, physiology, and health. Journal of Personality and Social Psychology, 63(2), 221-233. https://doi.org/10.1037/0022-3514.63.2.221

Gottman, J. M., & Levenson, R. W. (2000). The timing of divorce: Predicting when a couple will divorce over a 14-year period. Journal of Marriage and Family, 62(3), 737-745. https://doi.org/10.1111/j.1741-3737.2000.00737.x

Gross, J. J. (1998). The emerging field of emotion regulation: An integrative review. Review of General Psychology, 2(3), 271-299. https://doi.org/10.1037/1089-2680.2.3.271

Gross, J. J. (2015). Emotion regulation: Current status and future prospects. Psychological Inquiry, 26(1), 1-26. https://doi.org/10.1080/1047840X.2014.940781

Haber, M. G., Cohen, J. L., Lucas, T., & Baltes, B. B. (2007). The relationship between self-reported received and perceived social support: A meta-analytic review. American Journal of Community Psychology, 39(1-2), 133-144. https://doi.org/10.1007/s10464-007-9100-9

Hayes, S. C., Strosahl, K. D., & Wilson, K. G. (2012). Acceptance and commitment therapy: The process and practice of mindful change (2nd ed.). Guilford Press.

Hobfoll, S. E. (1989). Conservation of resources: A new attempt at conceptualizing stress. American Psychologist, 44(3), 513-524. https://doi.org/10.1037/0003-066X.44.3.513

Lazarus, R. S., & Folkman, S. (1984). Stress, appraisal, and coping. Springer.

Luthans, F., Avolio, B. J., Avey, J. B., & Norman, S. M. (2007). Positive psychological capital: Measurement and relationship with performance and satisfaction. Personnel Psychology, 60(3), 541-572. https://doi.org/10.1111/j.1744-6570.2007.00083.x

Mikulincer, M., & Shaver, P. R. (2016). Attachment in adulthood: Structure, dynamics, and change (2nd ed.). Guilford Press.

Minuchin, S. (1974). Families and family therapy. Harvard University Press.

Papp, L. M., & Witt, N. L. (2010). Romantic partners' individual coping strategies and dyadic coping: Implications for relationship functioning. Journal of Family Psychology, 24(5), 551-559. https://doi.org/10.1037/a0020836

Randall, A. K., & Bodenmann, G. (2009). The role of stress on close relationships and marital satisfaction. Clinical Psychology Review, 29(2), 105-115. https://doi.org/10.1016/j.cpr.2008.10.004

Senge, P. M. (1990). The fifth discipline: The art and practice of the learning organization. Doubleday.

Smith, P. (2026). Exploring marital resilience through the lived experiences and perception of spousal support during events of shared stressors (Order No. 32669734) [Doctoral dissertation, Walden University]. ProQuest Dissertations & Theses Global.

Smith, P. (2026). Love under pressure: Marital resilience, spousal support, and the science of shared stress. Mind & Method Consulting.

Walsh, F. (2016). Strengthening family resilience (3rd ed.). Guilford Press.

Wells, J. L., Haase, C. M., Rothwell, E. S., Naugle, K. G., Otero, M. C., Brown, C. L., Lai, J., Chen, K.-H., Connelly, D. E., Grimm, K. J., Levenson, R. W., & Fredrickson, B. L. (2022). Positivity resonance in long-term married couples: Multimodal characteristics and consequences for health and longevity. Journal of Personality and Social Psychology, 123(5), 983-1003. https://doi.org/10.1037/pspi0000385

Xu, Y., & Burleson, B. R. (2001). Effects of sex, culture, and support type on perceptions of spousal social support: An assessment of the support gap hypothesis in early marriage. Human Communication Research, 27(4), 535-566. https://doi.org/10.1111/j.1468-2958.2001.tb00792.x

ABOUT THE AUTHOR

PRINCE-JAMES SMITH, PHD

Prince-James Smith, PhD, is a cognitive psychology scholar, behavioral science practitioner, business strategist, and entrepreneur whose work centers on translating psychological and behavioral principles into practical real-world solutions. He holds a PhD in Cognitive Psychology, a Master of Science in Psychology, a Master of Philosophy in Psychology, and a Bachelor of Science in Business Administration and Change Management.

Dr. Smith's professional background spans business analytics, entrepreneurship, human resources, behavioral intervention, and applied psychology. He has more than thirteen years of experience in business analytics, more than ten years of experience as a human resources manager, and more than a decade of entrepreneurial experience developing businesses from the ground up. His work has consistently focused on systems, decision-making, human behavior, personal development, and the practical application of psychology to everyday life.

His academic and professional interests have long centered on relationships, communication, resilience, and the ways individuals develop within interpersonal systems. His master's thesis focused on improving couple communication techniques, while his doctoral dissertation examined marital resilience through the lived experiences and perceptions of spousal support during events of shared stressors. This scholarly foundation informs his broader work on helping individuals and couples understand how relationships function under pressure and how intentional learning can strengthen long-term connection.

Dr. Smith's approach integrates cognitive psychology, behavioral science, business principles, systems thinking, and relationship research. He is especially interested in how shifting perception can change behavior, improve communication, and support resilience. Through his writing and professional work, he encourages readers to examine themselves and their relationships with clarity, responsibility, and practical intention.

The Love Under Pressure Workbook reflects Dr. Smith's commitment to bridging academic knowledge and real-life application. It was created for individuals and couples who want more than inspiration. It was created for readers who are willing to study the patterns of love, practice repair, build shared vision, and continue learning how to show up with purpose.

www.ingramcontent.com/pod-product-compliance
Lightning Source LLC
LaVergne TN
LVHW060043210926
848481LV00013B/3940
* 9 7 9 8 9 9 6 2 2 6 2 4 5 *